THE HUMOR ISSUE

Where we laugh,
crack jokes, write
limericks, and revel
in the surprising,
the silly, and
the unexpected...

FROM US TO YOU...
the HUMOR issue

In place of the traditional LETTER FROM THE EDITOR page, we bring you a sampling from all our contributors.

OUR CONTRIBUTORS ANSWER A POLL:
WHAT IS YOUR FAVORITE JOKE?

Q: What is a cow's favorite thing to do on a Friday night?

A: Go to the moooovies.

DANIEL LABROSSE

YUK FUN

Q: How do you make a sausage roll?

A: Push it down a hill.

Q: Knock, knock.
A: Who's there?
Q: Banana.
A: Banana who?

(Continue until the person gets annoyed and then finally...)

Q: Knock, knock.
A: Who's there?
Q: Orange.
A: Orange who?
Q: Orange you glad I didn't say banana?

MUZZY

Q: Did you hear that I didn't get the job at the zoo?

Q: They said I wasn't Koala-fied.

SHAREE MILLER

Q: Why was the math book sad?

A: He had a lot of problems.

K-FAI STEELE

JESSIXA BAGLEY

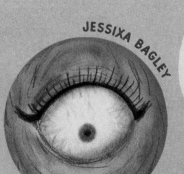

Q: What do you call a cow with three legs?

A: Lean beef.

AARON BAGLEY

Q: Why didn't the skeleton cross the road?

A: It didn't have the guts.

Q: What letter is always wet?

A: The C.

ALEJANDRA OVIEDO

GRACIAS

TOM BINGHAM

MIKE CURATO

Q: Where do cupcakes go on vacation?

A: A dessert island.

CHARLOTTE AGER

Q: What did the frog order at McDonald's?

A: French fries and a Diet Croak.

Q: What kind of shoes do frogs wear?

A: Open-toad sandals.

Q: Why do cows wear bells?

A: Because their horns don't work.

JACOB KAHN

Q: What happened when the vampire tried to write a poem?

A: Things went from bat to verse.

DAVID HUANG

JULIE BENBASSAT

DARIN SHULER

Q: Why did the duck hide her fart in her math book?

A: Because it only gets opened on special equations.

Q: What is a dentist's favorite time?

A: Tooth hurty.

inside

iLLUSTORIA

MEET SPECIAL GUESTS

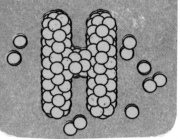

CHAPTER 1

LAUGH AND PLAY

GRAB A FRIEND & TRY THESE!

CHAPTER 2

READ AND LEARN

CHAPTER 3

DRAW, WRITE, MAKE

THE HUMOR ISSUE

CHAPTER 4

LOOK AND LISTEN

EXTRAS

TAKE A DEEPER DIVE

**ILLUSTORIA IS THE
OFFICIAL PUBLICATION
OF THE INTERNATIONAL
ALLIANCE OF YOUTH
WRITING CENTERS**

YUK FUNNIES
BY YUK FUN
WHAT DO YOU GET WHEN YOU CROSS A SNAKE WITH A TASTY DESSERT? A PIE-THON!
CACKLE
HYUK
SNORT
HAHA
TEE HEE
SSSO FUNNY!
HEEEEEE

OUR CHAPTER PAGES IN THIS ISSUE FEATURE TYPOGRAPHICAL ART BY JESSE JACOBS.

CHAPTER 1
LAUGH AND PLAY

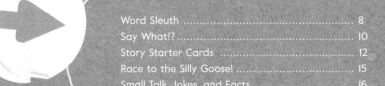

WORD SLEUTH

```
J C A C K L E Q K G
X G J W K L J L E I
P C H U C K L E L G
S F O E D R W R T G
C N R F K E A H R L
L D O V A K F O O E
K Z J R D C F W H Q
V R C K T I U L C B
K E L F R N G Z G Y
Y T C W W S N K I D
```

Flip to page 71 for the answers.

cackle   chuckle   snort   snicker
guffaw   chortle   giggle   howl

art by
DAVID
HUANG

SAY WHAT!?

art by Aaron Gonzalez

You are the apple of my... uh, eye bags!

What in the blue blazes? I mean, blue-green blazes.

Third time is a charm, but it really depends on the person.

Sssssooo, ssssshalll we make our own entertainment, now?

I know this color is outside my usual palette, but I'm going for it.

Just because I'm from the barnyard doesn't mean I don't know fashion!

MATCH THE SPEECH BUBBLE TO THE IMAGE.

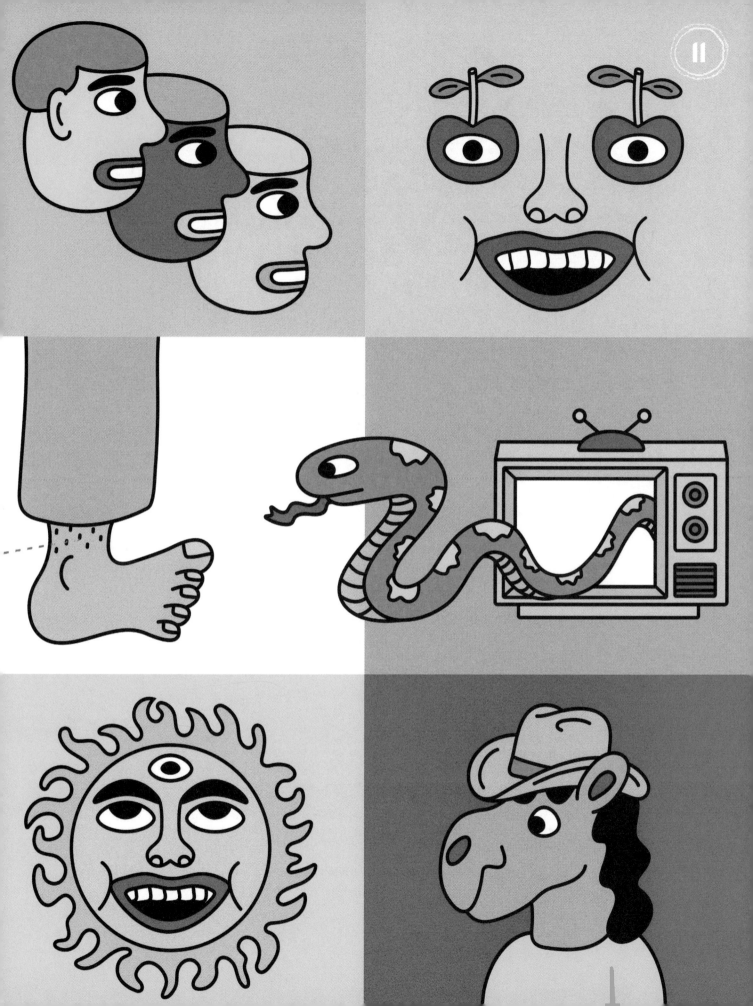

ABSURDIST WRITING
STORY STARTER CARDS
words by AMY SUMERTON   *art by* DANIEL LABROSSE

Daniel Labrosse is a self-taught artist working in Budapest, Hungary. He created these images from photographs he took and then digitally painted over. In this issue, we borrow from his silly brilliance and find the funny potential in boring, everyday moments.

INSTRUCTIONS

For this Story Starter exercise, you're invited to create wild scenes and irrational situations. Look at Daniel's artwork. He's taken decidedly un-exciting pictures (a city block, a stairwell, a trash bin, a pallet) and added strange elements to stoke the viewer's curiosity (and, perhaps, tickle their funny bone too).

When it comes to humor writing, be sure to expect the unexpected! Have you ever laughed at something just because it was so truly bizarre? In "absurdism," writers play with social norms to create character behaviors that intentionally make no sense. They take boring situations and transform them with weirdness.

STEPS

1. Cut out the four cards on the opposite page.

2. Pick a card and pretend you walked up to this scene. What's your first thought?

3. Pick up two cards. One card is your narrator, and the other is the scene they walked into. What do they think? How do they react? How do they interact?

4. Now take all four cards! What kind of wild, unexpected story can you create from all of these images? How can you tie them together into a cohesive, silly story?

EXTRA OBSERVATION QUESTIONS

What is happening? Who is responsible for this? Who discovers this? Why might this be happening? And, the tried-and-true best question any writer asks themselves, what happens next? And remember, keep it weird!

Finally! Take your own photo and draw or collage on top of it.
How can a boring moment become interesting?
Ask yourself: "What if....?" and go from there!

cut out cards on the other side

RACE TO THE SILLY GOOSE!

A hasty board game for bored people by Katharina Kulenkampff

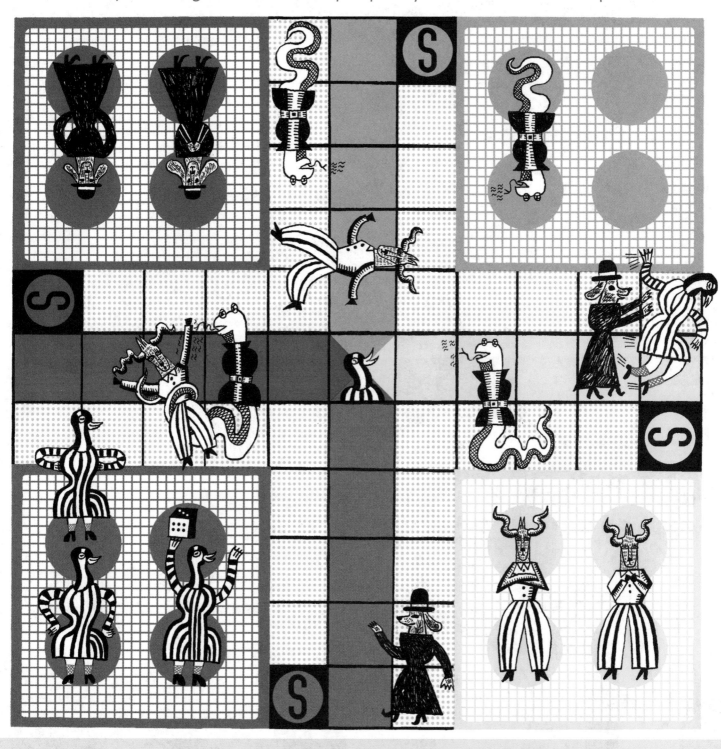

★ Get two, three, or four friends to play.
★ Find four snack items each, a different snack per person (such as cereal, jellybeans, grapes).
★ Pick a color corner. Put one snack on the "S" square, and the other three pieces in your corner.
★ Roll the dice to decide who starts. Whoever rolls the highest number goes first.

RULES

1. The goal of the game is to roll a number that adds up to six. Roll the dice only once each turn. Add your numbers together after every turn. Once you get to six, you can eat a snack!
2. If you roll a six you get an instant win.
3. When your snack reaches the center, you can eat it.
4. Repeat until all your snacks are gone!

JOKES + FACTS
by MUZZY
LAUGHTER IS SO INGRAINED IN HUMAN BRAINS THAT BABIES AS YOUNG AS SEVEN-TEEN DAYS OLD HAVE BEEN OBSERVED DOING IT.
JOKES ARE GOOD FOR YOU! SCIENTISTS HAVE FOUND THAT LAUGHING CAN IMPROVE IMMUNITY, HELP REGULATE BLOOD SUGAR LEVELS, AND IMPROVE SLEEP.
HUMANS AREN'T THE ONLY ONES THAT LAUGH. LAUGHTER AS COMMUNICATION IS FOUND IN OVER SIXTY SPECIES INCLUDING APES, RATS, AND DOLPHINS.

YUK FUNNIES
BY YUK FUN
WHAT DID THE SNAIL SAY AS HE RODE ALONG ON THE TURTLE'S BACK? "WHEEEE!"
SNICKER
HEHEHEH
HAH
HOWL
HAAAAAAA
ARF
TURTLE-Y HILARIOUS

TYPOGRAPHICAL ART BY JESSE JACOBS.

CHAPTER 2
READ AND LEARN

K-FAI STEELE WRITES AND ILLUSTRATES PICTURE BOOKS. SHE GREW UP IN A VERY OLD HOUSE IN MASSACHUSETTS WITH A PRINTING PRESS HER DAD BOUGHT FROM A MAGICIAN. SHE LIVES IN LAUSANNE, SWITZERLAND.

DARIN SHULER IS THE AUTHOR AND ILLUSTRATOR OF THE DOG & HAT SERIES. HE IS A MAJOR LEAGUE FART FACTORY.

MIKE CURATO IS AN ILLUSTRATOR AND AUTHOR OF CHILDREN'S BOOKS, INCLUDING THE LITTLE ELLIOT SERIES AND *WHERE IS BINA BEAR?*

WHY IS IT FUNNY?

ILLUSTRATED BY SHAREE MILLER

SOME THINGS MAKE US LAUGH AND WE DON'T KNOW WHY. LIKE SAYING THE WORDS "HOT DOG WATER." BUT SOME THINGS ACTUALLY DO HAVE A REASON FOR MAKING US LAUGH. DO YOU KNOW HOW SLIPPING ON A BANANA PEEL BECAME FUNNY?

IN THE LATE 19TH CENTURY, BANANAS BECAME A POPULAR IMPORTED FRUIT TO AMERICAN CITIES.

AT THAT TIME, MOST CITIES DIDN'T HAVE PUBLIC GARBAGE COLLECTION, SO PEOPLE WOULD JUST THROW THEIR TRASH OUT OF THE WINDOW ONTO THE STREETS BELOW!

A FAMOUS VAUDEVILLE ACTOR SAW A MAN ON THE SIDEWALK SLIP ON A BANANA PEEL. HE THOUGHT IT WAS SO FUNNY, HE TRIED IT ONSTAGE. IT BECAME SUCH A FAMOUS GAG, HE WAS NICKNAMED "SLIDING BILLY WATSON."

read and learn

THE GOOD, THE BAD, AND THE POTTY: ANATOMY OF HUMOR
ILLUSTRATED BY DARIN SHULER

LEARNING HOW THE BODY FUNCTIONS IS EDUCATIONAL. LEARNING HOW THE BODY DYSFUNCTIONS IS HUMERUS. (GET IT?) THE HUMERUS IS THE LONG BONE IN YOUR UPPER ARM. (IT'S NOT ACTUALLY AS FUNNY WHEN YOU EXPLAIN IT.)

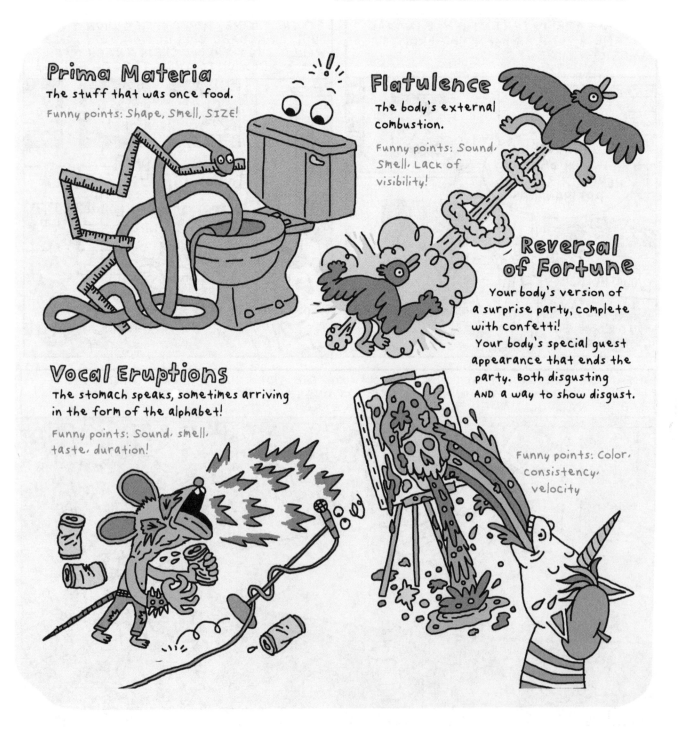

Prima Materia
The stuff that was once food.
Funny points: Shape, Smell, SIZE!

Flatulence
The body's external combustion.
Funny points: Sound, Smell, Lack of visibility!

Reversal of Fortune
Your body's version of a surprise party, complete with confetti!
Your body's special guest appearance that ends the party. Both disgusting AND a way to show disgust.
Funny points: Color, consistency, velocity

Vocal Eruptions
The stomach speaks, sometimes arriving in the form of the alphabet!
Funny points: Sound, smell, taste, duration!

THE NATURE OF HUMOR!
ILLUSTRATED BY K-FAI STEELE

HAVE YOU EVER SEEN A SEAGULL TRIP? I HAVE. IT'S HILARIOUS. THE BIRD PROBABLY DIDN'T EVEN REALIZE IT HAPPENED. PROOF THAT ANIMALS ARE FUNNY WITHOUT EVEN TRYING!

KANGAROOS LICK THEIR ARMS TO STAY COOL.

TURTLES CAN BREATHE THROUGH THEIR REAR ENDS.

HIPPOS SWEAT IS PINK AND ACTS LIKE SUNSCREEN.

read and learn

interview with

OUR COVER ARTIST
PIETER VAN EENOGE:

Pieter is an award-winning Belgian illustrator. His work has a strong narrative character, and he creates fantastic and surreal worlds in his images. He lives in Bruges with his wife, two sons, and a cat.

Q: TELL US ABOUT A BOOK FROM CHILDHOOD THAT STILL INFLUENCES YOU TODAY.

A: I grew up with Belgian and French comic books like Suske en Wiske, Jommeke, and Asterix. It was the 1980s and all the kids I knew read the same things. Life was easy and so were the books.

"Hunger is an emotion."

Q: DESCRIBE AN UNUSUAL OBJECT IN YOUR STUDIO.

A: A little frame with dried mountain flowers my mom picked in Switzerland some fourty years ago. There are two edelweiss flowers in it, a highly endangered species nowadays, and very forbidden to pick.

"A hug knot is the tightest knot of all."

Q: What's next on your artistic plate?

A: A large picture book about houses, one year as Museum Illustrator for Musea Brugge, and fixing the light above my desk.

read and learn

"my largest work of art yet — on a wall in the Belgian city of RONSE."

Q: WHAT DO YOU TELL YOURSELF WHEN YOU ARE IN THE MOST DIFFICULT PART OF THE CREATIVE PROCESS?

A: "Being an illustrator is still the best job in the world, so stop whining and put your back into it!"

Q: WHAT WOULD BE A DREAM PROJECT FOR YOU?

A: One where I don't have doubts, stress, headaches and imposter syndrome from start to finish.

"there's always work in progress lying around the studio."

Q: FAVORITE SNACK WHILE WORKING?

A: No snacks... Eating and painting isn't the best combination.

Q: MORNING PERSON OR NIGHT OWL?

A: Neither. I need a lot of sleep.

Q: ART SUPPLY YOU CAN'T LIVE WITHOUT?

A: Moulin du Roy paper by Canson.

Q: ALBUM LISTENED TO RECENTLY?

A: *The Lamb Lies Down on Broadway.* 1970s Genesis at its best!

PICTURALE '22

PIETER VAN EENOGE

WE ASKED A POET...

JACOB KAHN IS A POET LIVING IN THE BAY AREA. WE GAVE HIM AN ARTICLE TO READ ABOUT THE BIOLOGY OF LAUGHTER*. HERE ARE HIS THOUGHTS.

What's the longest you've ever laughed for? Maybe thirty minutes, an hour? How about sixteen straight days? Apparently, this can happen. It's called laughing disease. And you don't get it just because something is funny. Or maybe it starts out that way. You and your friends find something hilarious, or weird, or awkward, and so one of you starts laughing and then another, but soon no one can stop.

Trying to stop makes the laughter even more intense. You can't look at each other. You can't talk without bursting out. One of you gets the hiccups because of the convulsions. Another is crying in pain, "Stop! I can't take it!"

Now, you're laughing at that. This goes on and on. And it's worse if

you're in public, maybe at school, or at a restaurant. People are looking at you. Your laughter is confusing them, they're like, "What are you laughing at?" or, "What is so funny?" But even they start smiling and laughing. Laughing because other people are laughing. Things have gone off the rails. Is this even laughter anymore, or is it some sort of spell, a contagion?

Whether it's a quick giggle or a case of laughing disease, laughter is a form of expression, like language. We can say things in laughter that maybe we can't say with words. Or that can't be said better any other way. Things like, "Wow, it is so nice to hang out with you, we have so much in common, our minds are so alike!" Or, like, "Can you believe

*"WHY DO HUMANS LAUGH? THE EVOLUTIONARY BIOLOGY OF LAUGHTER." VISIT P. 71 FOR MORE INFO.

how hard and boring everything is right now?" You can celebrate with laughter, connect with laughter, flirt with laughter, stall with laughter, manipulate with laughter, complain with laughter, revolt with laughter.

Laughter is like silly putty, it can take any shape. Researchers have tried to make sensible graphs about when and why people laugh, and eighty percent of the time people don't even laugh in response to something funny. They do it to punctuate conversation, because they see a friend, or because they think they should. People hardly laugh when they are alone.

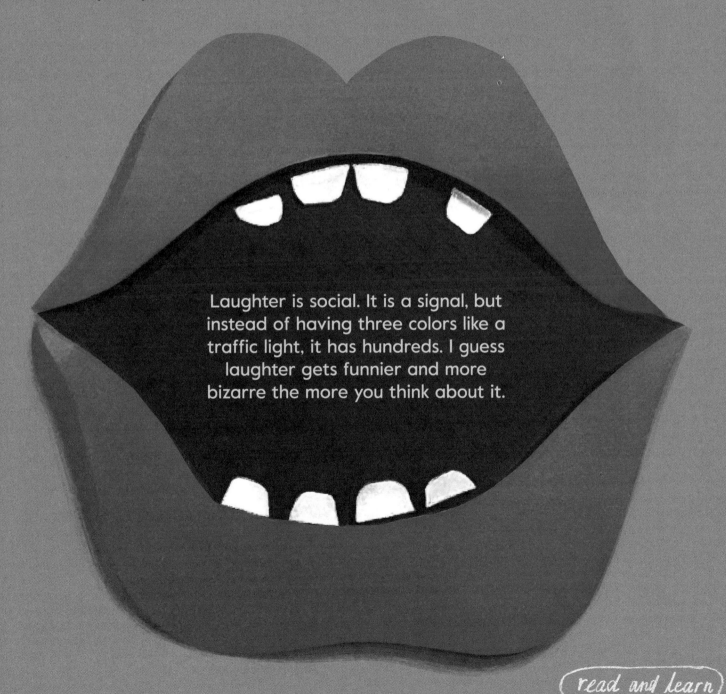

Laughter is social. It is a signal, but instead of having three colors like a traffic light, it has hundreds. I guess laughter gets funnier and more bizarre the more you think about it.

CREATURE FEATURE

words by Amy Sumerton // art by Julie Benbassat

Greetings, humans! Doc Anthurium, here.

Scientist and, ahem, *actual flower*, here to check out the latest looks making waves on the red, erm, green, carpet! Birds use all kinds of avian fashions to stand out on beaches, in forests, and yes, of course, the air!

Birds of Paradise know: It's all about the accessories! These ornithological wonders sure know how to stand out in the theater of the tropical forest. There are fourty-five different species of this type of bird—and all of them accessorize differently, from elaborate, brightly colored plumage, to iridescent neck feathers.

Funny feet, funny name, funny little birds! The blue legs and feet really enhance the strut of these charming creatures.

Perhaps you've seen them in the hit comedies *Great Galapagos!* or *Save the Last Cute Mating Dance for Me.*

Regardless, you'll be sure to see lots of blue on the Pacific runways this season!

Speaking of accessories, look at the kicks on these birds! No—I'm not talking about their feet—I'm talking about their beaks!

Shoebills—which are believed to be descendants of actual dinosaurs—are named for their huge, clog-like beaks.

Their impressive size (up to five feet tall!) stands out, but on the runway, these silent, solitary birds prefer to walk alone.

And check out the dapper knickers on the secretary bird! They really accentuate the long leg-line on these stork-like creatures.

Unique in looks and behavior, secretary birds are the only terrestrial birds of prey!

But these fashionistas know that knickers alone do not make a look, so they top it off with a sassy fascinator hat.

Très chic!

read and learn

CREATING FUNNY CHARACTERS with DASHA TOLSTIKOVA

DASHA IS A PICTURE BOOK AUTHOR AND ILLUSTRATOR LIVING IN BROOKLYN, NEW YORK. SOME OF HER BOOKS FEATURE UNEXPECTED HEROES— LIKE A MISBEHAVING CHAIR AND A TINY, JUSTICE-SEEKING ONION. WE WANTED TO KNOW MORE!

Before we ask about your newest book, *The Adventures of Cipollino*, tell us a little bit about *The Bad Chair*.
The Bad Chair is a story about a friendship triangle between a real girl, her favorite stuffed Monkey, and an anthropomorphized chair. The three play a nightly game, until Monkey goes missing.

It is an ode to my love of anthropomorphic* objects and also to the very real complexity of having a close friendship between three people.

The book started with me considering a favorite lost toy (Monkey) and then musing on what if Monkey is not just lost but in fact abducted by someone (Chair!) who is trying to keep Monkey away because he is jealous.

*anthropomorphic (adjective)
having human characteristics.

A cipollino is a type of tiny onion shaped like a flying saucer. Can you tell us the origin story of this unlikely hero? *The Adventures of Cipollino* is an Italian book, first published in 1951. It was hugely popular in the Soviet Union (where I grew up) for decades and was my father's childhood favorite in the early 1960s as well as as mine in the 1980s. The book is about class struggle, where anthropomorphized (draw what you know, they say!) vegetables rise up to overthrow their cruel fruit overlords.

GIANNI RODARI

Adventures of
CIPOLLINO

illustrated by
DASHA TOLSTIKOVA

read and learn

What artistic strategies did you use to give the vegetables their own personalities?
I've been reading and re-reading the book since before I could remember, so I have been thinking about their personalities for decades. I wanted the look to be Italian, but not specifically, and for fashion inspiration, looked to the period between the world wars. Some of the outfits are a bit out of time.

For instance, there are two Countesses of The Cherry Tree and one wears a peach colored pant suit with a neckerchief, while her sister is always in a flapper-like dress and small booties. The working class vegetables wear a lot of chore jackets and sometimes fun-colored socks.

Did you ever think that you'd grow up to be an artist who paints lemons in armor riding on cucumber horses?
Let's just say I couldn't have imagined I would be so lucky! But not entirely surpised. I spent most of my childhood drawing epic stick figure tales in sketchbooks.

What else did you think you'd grow up to be when you were a kid?
I always wanted to be a writer. But I also dreamed of being a lounge singer in long red velvet dresses. Unfortunately, I am pretty tone deaf.

Have you ever thought of a book idea that is too strange to publish?
Oh my gosh! Most of my ideas! I am pondering something called *The Spoon Thief* at the moment, so stand by.

Were any of the characters difficult to develop?
Esquire Peapod, the turncoat lawyer, was hard to draw. At first I thought he was going to be a pea—a round character—but then I realized he was a peaPOD. So not entirely round.

And I must say drawing Cip himself (that's my nickname for Cipollino) was hard. He needed to be smart and kind and good but also not entirely sweet. I wanted him to have spunk. It's surprisingly hard to get all of these characteristics down at once!

Who were your favorite characters to draw?
I suppose I do have a soft spot in my heart for Count Maraschino, the Countesses' nephew, who is bookish and terribly mistreated by his aunts. In the end, he comes into his own and helps the vegetables in their quest.

What fuels your art making process?
Dried bananas and gummy bears.

Background music?
Currently I am in a French pop phase, but mostly I have dramas about teens in trouble in the background while I paint.

Is there a difficult color that you avoid?
Green! I hate green!

Other artists you're inspired by?
MB Goffstein, Nellie Mae Rowe, Ruth Asawa, Amy Sillman, Carson Ellis, Cátia Chien, Gracie Zhang, and Weng Pixin.

read and learn

Vivian Pham is a Vietnamese-Australian author and teacher. Her work focuses on feminism, racism, and the Vietnamese diaspora.

YOUTH activist

"Remember that you make the world a beautiful place simply by seeing it that way."

In 2017, Vivian wrote her debut young-adult novel *The Coconut Children* with Story Factory, a nonprofit youth writing center in Sydney, Australia. Find it at a book-store near you.

WHAT IS THE MOST SURPRISING THING YOU'VE LEARNED TEACHING FOR STORY FACTORY?

I've learned that being a good listener is a very important part of being a good teacher. It's especially useful when you're trying to create a space for students to feel confident sharing their writing!

WHERE DO YOU FIND INSPIRATION?

In other people. Sometimes they happen to be other writers, but mostly I am inspired by people who are generous, kind, brave, funny, and like to point out the beauty in simple things.

PHOTOS BY JACQUIE MANNING

VIVIAN DELIVERING A CREATIVE WRITING WORKSHOP BASED ON *THE COCONUT CHILDREN* IN A WESTERN SYDNEY HIGH SCHOOL.

A Day in the Life of
DUST BUNNY AND PILL BUG

By Jaia Linden-Engel

read and learn

YUK FUNNIES
BY YUK FUN
WHAT'S THE BEST WAY TO COOK A GATOR? IN A CROCK POT!
HA HA
GUFFAW
HOHO
CHORTLE
LOL
WAIT, WHAT?
HEHEHE

CHAPTER 3

DRAW WRITE MAKE

TYPOGRAPHICAL ART BY JESSE JACOBS.

MAKE THIS

POP-UP UN-BIRTHDAY CARD

YOU NEED:

SCRAP PAPER
GLUE STICK / TAPE
MARKERS, PENCILS

An absurd idea proposed by the Mad Hatter in Lewis Carroll's *Alice in Wonderland*. Surprise an unsuspecting friend with one of these cards!

1. Fold two pieces of paper in half. Draw a line from the folded edge.

2. Cut along the line. Fold back the edge to make a triangle.

3. Repeat with the other edge. Open card and pop the shapes through.

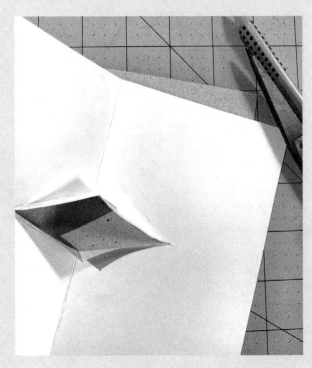

DO YOU KNOW WHAT *day* IT IS

4. Glue the pop out card to the colored paper, draw your animal around the mouth, and add words.

5. Create the front of the card, hinting at a surprise. Add color with marker, pencils, or collage.

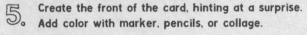

Try different animals: birds with big or small beaks, frogs with giant mouths, cats, and dogs. As you open and shut the card, the mouth appears to be talking!

43

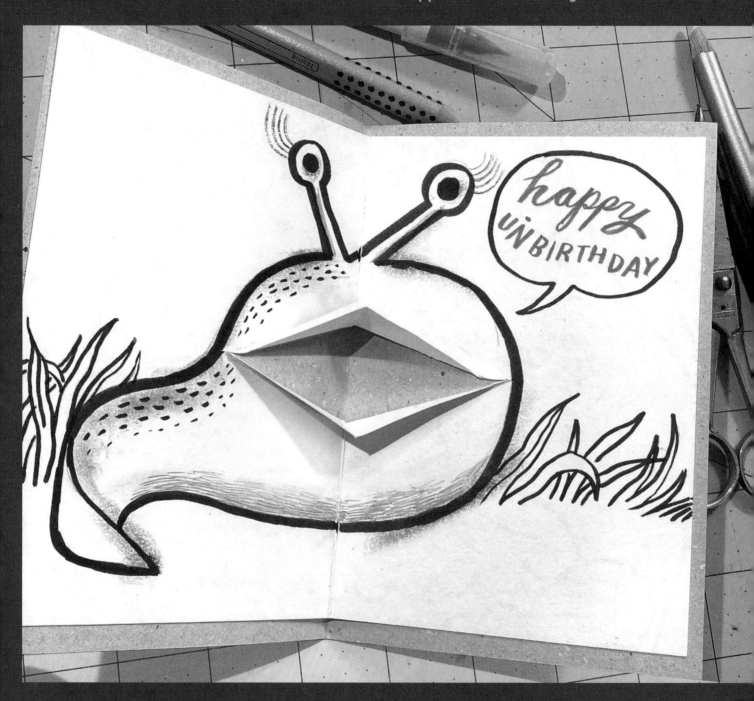

Every single day of the year that is **NOT** your birthday is therefore your **UN-BIRTHDAY.**

So you have 364 possible days out of the year on which you could plan such a party. Get going!

draw, write, make

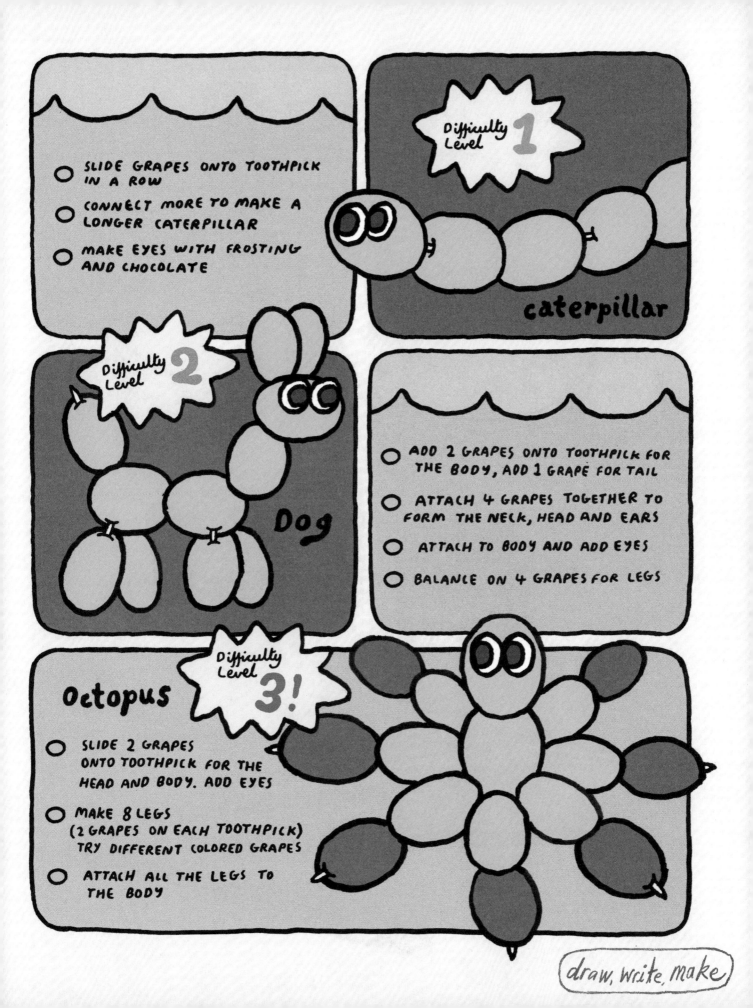

Absurdist Q & A

This collaborative writing game was a favorite of the Surrealist artists. Play with as many friends as you can get to join!

YOU NEED:

SCRAP PAPER, CANS, JARS, MARKERS, PENCILS

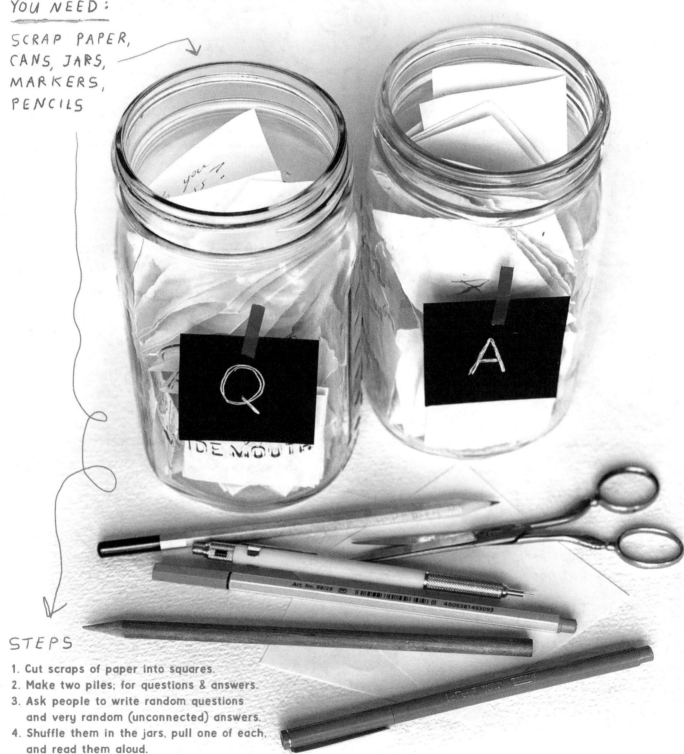

STEPS

1. Cut scraps of paper into squares.
2. Make two piles; for questions & answers.
3. Ask people to write random questions and very random (unconnected) answers.
4. Shuffle them in the jars, pull one of each, and read them aloud.

WHAT FITS INSIDE OUR CUSTOM TOTE BAG?

GUNK
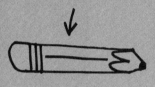

YOUR TINY DOG?

FAVORITE ART SUPPLIES
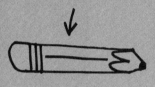

YOUR GRANDMA?

THE BEST MAGAZINES

HAVE YOU SUBSCRIBED YET?*

(check all that apply)

- [ ] Yes, but now I need a gift subscription for my grandma's cousin's nephew.
- [ ] No, I can do that after I finish eating my cereal.
- [ ] I swear I will as soon as I finish this headstand.

*While you're at it, why not also grab a tote?

STORE.MCSWEENEYS.NET

Daniel's self portrait, as seen in his studio in Budapest.

DRAW THIS— DOODLE-FACE portrait

This idea is brought to you by artist Daniel Labrosse.
Are these self portraits? Or portraits of total strangers?
Try this out on someone you know. Give one as a funny present!

STEPS:

① draw the neck area and shoulders

② clothing details
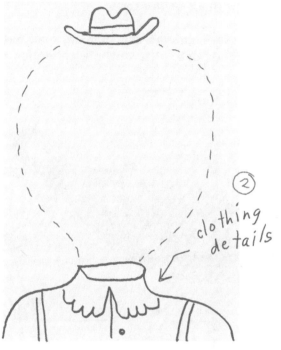

③ fill in with doodles
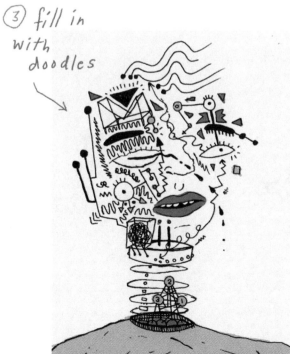

④ Add eyes and ears? Maybe NOT?

draw, write, make

WRITE THIS — LIMERICK

Are you famililar with the limerick, a form of funny poetry? Edward Lear made this rhyming format popular with his book *The Book of Nonsense*.

Read these examples and then try one. Get together with some friends and write a whole collection of silly tales.

EDWARD LEAR ILLUSTRATES HIS OWN POEMS IN *THE BOOK OF NONSENSE*.

THERE WAS AN OLD MAN WITH A BEARD,
WHO SAID, "IT IS JUST AS I FEARED!—
TWO OWLS AND A HEN,
FOUR LARKS AND A WREN,
HAVE ALL BUILT THEIR NESTS IN MY BEARD.

THERE WAS A YOUNG LADY WHOSE BONNET
CAME UNTIED WHEN THE BIRDS SAT UPON IT
BUT SHE SAID "I DON'T CARE!
ALL THE BIRDS IN THE AIR,
ARE WELCOME TO SIT ON MY BONNET!"

There was a young lady whose bonnet, Came untied when the birds sate But she said, "I don't care! — All the birds in the air are welcome to set on my bonnet!"

YOU TRY

THERE ONCE WAS A _____ NAMED _____

WHO WANTED TO _____.

HE/SHE/IT/THEY (VERB)_____ ON A (NOUN) _____,

AND SAID, "WHAT A _____!"

AND THEN _____.

DRAWN BY YOU

PROMPT: Draw your funniest face!

Rocco,
age 8,
Paranaque City,
Philippines

Charlie,
age 6,
Copenhagen, Denmark

Baxter, age 8,
Seattle, Washington

Nyella,
age 8,
Seattle,
Washington

Connor,
age 6,
Houston,
Texas

Alma,
age 8,
Mostova, Slovakia

Claudia,
age 8,
Becici, Montenegro

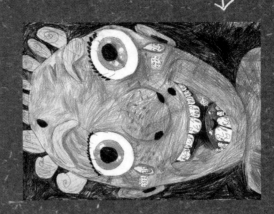

Anthony,
age 12,
Strasbourg, France

Polina,
age 14,
Moscow, Russia

Emilio, age 11,
Córdoba, Argentina

Follow our newsletter to hear about upcoming
calls for youth artwork submissions!

draw, write, make

THERE ONCE WAS A TROPICAL MONKEY,
WHO LIKED HER BANANAS ALL CHUNKY.
TO SWING ON A VINE
WAS, TO HER, ONLY FINE,
BECAUSE SOMETIMES SHE MISSED THE TREE'S TRUNKY.

youth writing

WE ASKED STUDENTS TO WRITE THEIR OWN LIMERICK.

DEFYING GRAVITY

from 916 INK in SACRAMENTO, CALIFORNIA
A MEMBER OF THE INTERNATIONAL ALLIANCE OF YOUTH WRITERS

written by DOMINIC FISCHER, age 15
art by CHARLOTTE AGER

A man told a girl not to fly,
It would be better if she baked a pie.
She sighed in annoyance,
For he lacked flamboyance.
Then she took off and soared through the sky.

CHAPTER 4

LOOK AND LISTEN

Picked by
JESSIXA BAGLEY,
our guest curator
in this issue.

This was my FAVORITE album to listen to as a kid. I've listened to it SO many times.

LISTEN TO OUR FULL PLAYLIST FOR THIS ISSUE ON SPOTIFY. USE THIS QR CODE TO DELVE INTO AN HOUR OF EAR-TINGLING TUNES... THE PERFECT BACKDROP TO JUMP INTO ONE OF OUR DIY PROJECTS FROM CHAPTER 3!

OIL PASTELS
I love the way it glides on paper and the line stands out.

ON OUR DESK:

Selected by one of our favorite artists to work with, ALEJANDRA OVIEDO.

CHARCOAL AND ERASER
This duo is perfect for creating textures and combining different shades. I make a charcoal surface with my finger and with the eraser I draw on it. Crazy, right? The eraser in this case is my drawing tool.

SCISSORS AND COLORED PAPER
I like to make not-so-perfect shapes to add to my illustrations to bring them to life.

GOUACHE
I find this technique very versatile that allows me to make translucent or opaque paintings, it also has very beautiful bright colors, creating illustrations with a lot of texture and color.

FAVORITE SNACK
A bowl of greek yogurt with blueberries, nuts, and chocolate chips.

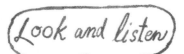

Look and listen

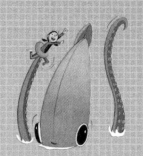

LAUGH ALONG WITH THE ODDBALLS!

A giant squid! Rats in bowler hats! Synchronised swimming! Bao! Dodos! Meet Agnes, Roberta, and Ruby – self-described oddballs with a nose for adventure!

The Adventures of Team Pom
—Squid Happens

The Adventures of Team Pom
—The Last Dodo

The Adventures of Team Pom feature a host of incredible characters set against a background of Queens, New York. Follow our three friends as they stumble upon mystery after mystery in their home neighbourhoods, and chaos follows as the team are met by dastardly villains in increasingly slapstick scenarios.

"NONSTOP ACTION AND SLAPSTICK HUMOUR... JOYFULLY ABSURD"
—PUBLISHERS WEEKLY

Published by Flying Eye Books
www.flyingeyebooks.com

♪ 𝗳 ⬛ 𝕏 ⬛ @FlyingEyeBooks

Subtly Humorous Picture Books
for ages 3 to 7

A quirky and hilarious parable about parental distraction and a daughter's clever solution.

When Grandma moves in, a precocious child shares her witty tips for making her feel at home.

A collection of amusing and sweet picture books featuring adorable forest friends.

For resources including downloadable materials, please visit www.tundrabooks.com

WE ASKED YOU TO TELL US ABOUT YOUR FAVORITE FUNNY BOOK

BOOK REVIEW

CONTEST

IF YOU LAUGH, I'm starting THIS BOOK OVER!

BY Chris Harris

Illustrated by carae Ron

by. **Spike, age 6, Houston, Texas**

If You Laugh, I'm Starting This Book Over by Chris Harris

It's a really funny book and it will make you laugh so hard. The author calls you a fifty-six-year-old dentist and a pineapple wearing children's clothes! There's only one rule... Do. Not. Laugh!!!

by **Aurelia, age 10,**
Warsaw, Poland

Diary of a Wimpy Kid:
The Long Haul
by Jeff Kinney

1. This book is so funny
it will give you laughing
gas for a long time.

2. Read this book
after a hard school or
work day. It will make
everything better.

by **Agatha, age 9**
Polskie Łąki, Poland

Zu dę daś
the Polish edition of:
Du Iz Tak
by Carson Ellis

I got this book for my
birthday and I love it! You
can always guess what the
worms are talking about.
And you can always find
something new because
there is always something
you haven't seen before!

What If? 2
by Randall Munroe

I like Randall Munroe's *What If? 2* because it's comedic, scientific, and zany. It's perfect for science lovers who want a bit of a laugh. I love it because of its crazy questions and impossible comedy. I also really like the illustrations. The stick figures are somehow really realistic!

by   **Sage, age 10**

Ithaca, New York

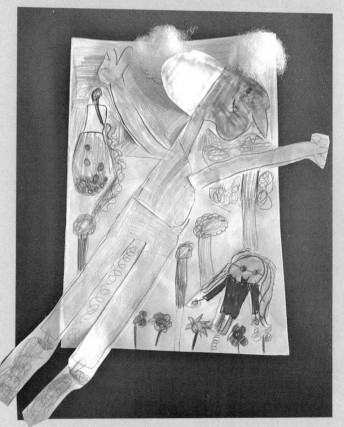

The BFG
(short for The Big Friendly Giant)
by Roald Dahl

I thought it was funny when the BFG was talking about the snozcumber and when he fluffed in the Queen's face. This is exactly what happened. The BFG was drinking frobscottle and saw the Queen. The BFG bowed and said your majesty. Suddenly there was a loud FLUFF. The Queen was surprised. She lifted her hands and said "GOODNESS ME". In the meantime the BFG rose higher and higher in to the air because of the enormous powerful fluff!

by   **Rhia, age 7**

Flintshire, Wales

Rosie dreams of forests, meadows, hares, and freedom. Trapped at the race-track, she sprints in endless circles – until one day, Rosie makes a fearless beeline for the enormous world beyond the track...

The artwork of *Rosie Runs* is the wildest Maijala so far!
—Rudolf Koivu Prize jury

MARIKA MAIJALA

ROSIE RUNS

TRANSLATED BY MIA SPANGENBERG

Claude Ponti

HĪZNOBYŪTĪ

Translated from the French by Alyson Waters

Claude Ponti

My Valley

Translated from the French by Alyson Waters

ROSIE RUNS

MARIKA MAIJALA
TRANSLATED BY MIA SPANGENBERG
August 15, 2023

My Valley and *Hīznobyūtī*
translated by
Alyson Waters
now in paperback

elsewhere editions
www.elsewhereeditions.org
distributed to the trade
by Penguin Random House

ON OUR BOOKSHELF

Albert is a magical talking pudding who, no matter how often he is eaten, always reforms in order to be eaten again. Made in 1918!

-by
NORMAN LINDSAY

Step inside the world's strangest school and meet all the eccentric characters inside.

-by
LOUIS SACHAR
& ADAM MACCAULEY

Super funny series about disgusting creatures! Or are they just misunderstood?

-by
BOB SHEA &
ZACHARIAH OHORA

This book is funny because... I mean, look at the title. Need we say more?

-by
ELISE GRAVEL

Other creatures featured in this series: Worm, Mosquito, Toad, Bat, Cockroach, and Head Lice. You're gonna want 'em as pets!

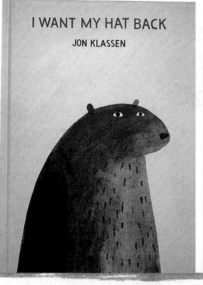

I WANT MY HAT BACK

JON KLASSEN

Extremely subtle, understated humor. Check out the series!

Hilarious snack-able adventures! You'll never look at your dinner plate the same way again.

-by JARRETT LERNER

A GRAPHIC NOVEL CHAPTER BOOK

THE HUNGER HEROES

Missed Meal Mayhem

Jarrett Lerner

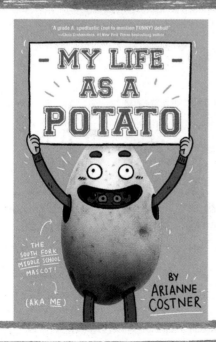

"A grade A spudtastic (not to mention FUNNY) debut!"
—Chris Grabenstein, #1 New York Times bestselling author

- MY LIFE - AS A POTATO

THE SOUTH FORK MIDDLE SCHOOL MASCOT!

(A.K.A. ME)

BY ARIANNE COSTNER

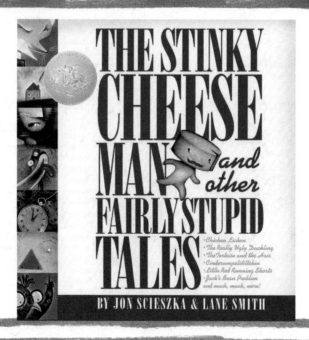

THE STINKY CHEESE MAN and other FAIRLY STUPID TALES

·Chicken Licken
·The Really Ugly Duckling
·The Tortoise and the Hair
·Cinderumpelstiltskin
·Little Red Running Shorts
·Jack's Bean Problem
and much, much, more!

BY JON SCIESZKA & LANE SMITH

-by
ARIANNE COSTNER

Imagine you are a potato! What is your life like? Super silly, read out loud-able.

-by
JON SCIESZKA
& LANE SMITH

A side-splitting reinvention of classic children's tales.

Look and listen

STINKY fun with Laurence King Publishing!

Make the story your own, draw a line with a twist—
the picture is YOURS to paint!

Enchanted Lion Books
BROOKLYN, NY

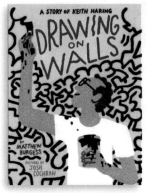

Drawing on Walls

This BIG, joyful picture book biography of the beloved Keith Haring celebrates the transformative power of art. Readers of all ages will be propelled to pick up a pencil or paintbrush of their own!

Telling Stories Wrong

"Once upon a time, there was a girl called Little Yellow Riding Hood—" "Not yellow! It's RED Riding Hood!" Readers will enjoy this exuberant recounting of a well-known fairytale, as a spirited granddaughter & grandfather improvise back and forth!

Make Meatballs Sing

Fired up by the social justice causes of her day, artist & educator Corita Kent was a nun like no other! Pick up this vibrant biography for an invitation to make & see anew. As Corita liked to say, "There is no win and no fail. There's only MAKE."

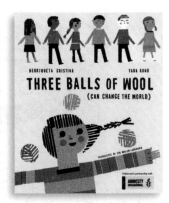

Three Balls of Wool (Can Change the World)

In a conformist society, a mom unravels her kids' monochrome sweaters to create BOLD, colorful patterns! This powerful picture book centers creativity as the beating heart of both courage & change.

enchantedlion.com • @enchantedlion

Deeper Dive!

...CONTINUED FROM PAGE 30
WE ASKED A POET

Read about the biological function of laughter in scientific detail in the article we gave poet Jacob Kahn called, **"Why Do Humans Laugh? The Evolutionary Biology of Laughter,"** written by Peter McGraw and Joel Warner. Find it on Slate.com. March 25, 2014.

...CONTINUED FROM PAGE 32
CREATURE FEATURE

You've simply got to see these birds in action! We highly recommend watching David Attenborough's documentary series called **The Life of Birds**. One episode features styles of nesting, another focuses on varieties of eggs, and the most entertaining one (if we have a favorite) is the one about mating dances. Ask for it at your local library or read about it at PBS.ORG/lifeofbirds/sirdavid.

...CONTINUED FROM PAGE 35
INTERVIEW WITH DASHA TOLSTIKOVA

Other books illustrated by Dasha Tolstikova: **A Year Without Mom**, **Violet and the Woof**, and **Friend or Foe?**.

Read more by Gianni Rodari, an Italian writer most famous for his works of children's literature (akin to our Dr. Seuss, regarding scope of influence and level of absurdity). Check out these collections of short stories: **Telephone Tales**, illustrated by Valerio Vidali, and **Telling Stories Wrong**, illustrated by Beatrice Alemagna.

...CONTINUED FROM PAGE 50
WRITE THIS: LIMERICK

Find more fascinating facts from **Edward Lear and the Mysterious Origin of Limericks**, written by Fred Hornaday, on KingofLimericks.com.

The annual **Bring Your Limericks to Limerick** competition began in 2013 at the University of Limerick and continues to this day.

The limerick evolved over centuries to become a type of poetry that defied logical understanding. Nonsense verse grew in popularity during the Victorian era after Edward Lear's **The Book of Nonsense** was published in 1846.

Perhaps the strictly controlled behavior of the era caused readers to crave goofy and rebellious forms of poetry?

```
J C A C K L E Q K G
X G J W K L J L E I
P C H U C K L E L G
S F O E D R W R T G
C N R F K E A H R L
L D Q V A K F O O E
K Z J R D C F W H Q
V R C K T I U L C B
K E L F R N G Z G Y
Y T C W W S N K I D
```

Answer key for the Word Sleuth on page 9.

THE YOUTH WRITING IN THIS ISSUE IS BY STUDENTS FROM:

916 Ink in Sacramento, California

TAKE A TRIP AND VISIT!

FIND A WRITING CENTER NEAR YOU: ➤ YOUTHWRITING.ORG

In every issue of *Illustoria*, students from the The International Alliance of Youth Writing Centers contribute their own writing and art to add a range of voices to these pages. The International Alliance is joined in a common belief that young people need places where they can write and be heard, where they can have their voices polished, published, and amplified. There are nearly seventy centers worldwide. Learn more at www.youthwriting.org.